My Bones Being Wiser

my Bones

Middletown, Connecticut

BEING WISER

Poems by
VASSAR MILLER

WESLEYAN UNIVERSITY PRESS

Library of Congress Catalog Card Number: 63-17793
Manufactured in the United States of America
First Edition

For Jeff

Contents

My Bones Being Wiser

Invitation

Here is the land where children
Feel snows that never freeze,
Where a star's the reflection
Of a baby's eyes,

Where both wise men and shepherds
Measure all Heaven no smaller
Nor larger than He is
And judge a lamb is taller,

Where old and cold for proof
Would take a stone apart,
Who find a wisp of hay
Less heavy on the heart

Come near the cradle where
The Light on hay reposes,
Where hands may touch the Word
This winter warm with roses.

Precision

The leaves blow speaking
green, lithe words
in no man's language.

Although I would
translate them—better
living in silence,

letting the leaves
breathe through me all men's
in no man's language.

Hot Air

So soft my pleasure came
Upon a dream,
Iced fire and frosted flame

It was, too brief for blame.
Yet sharp to seem
So soft. My pleasure came

And went—that was its shame,
Not that, supreme,
Iced fire and frosted flame,

It bore the ancient name
Harsh hearts blaspheme.
So soft my pleasure, came

A wind and woke me tame
To that regime
Iced fire and frosted flame

Had burnt to a black frame
Before their steam.
So soft, my pleasure, came
Iced fire and frosted flame.

13

Reverent Impiety

I will not fast, for I have fasted longer
Than forty days and known a leaner Lent
Than can be kept with ceremonial hunger,
Since life's a lengthier season to repent
Than the brief time when spring's first winds may tease
The ashes on the brow, when bird songs intercept
The misereres chanted on our knees,
And ritual tears that I such hours have wept
Mirror a double and a muddy vision
That would not win a blessing from a priest.
Hence, purity born from my pain's precision
Refuses here to fast upon a feast,
Glutted till now on sacraments of air,
Memorials to loves that never were.

Poor Relations

Grief was your proper privilege, so awful
No one attained it, held by you alone
An honor for the likes of me unlawful
Because I had no loss to call my own
Except the losing of such trivial things
People disdained even to notice it—
A broken doll, strayed kittens, lost tin rings,
An angry playmate, or a nurse who quit.
These mattered but as matters for your scorn
Muffled in smiles or frowns, for how dare measure
Your love that died with my love never born!
And thus you taught me not to touch your treasure.
And thus, a poor relation by your bier,
I scarcely have a penny of a tear.

Heritage

I wake up early,
the day spread out before me, blank, like a sheet of paper,
and I have nothing to write
but your name.

I wake up early,
the humid air around me is a listening ear,
and I have nothing to say
but your name.

I speak it aloud,
but your name loosed from my lips is dry like a sparrow's cheep,
having little to do
with either of us.

Let me recall
how many have waked up early and found loneliness waiting
like a small beast from the woods
made a pet,

which, when it grew up,
for all that they had coaxed it with words or with work,
would turn wild again
and tear them

though it had worn
the shape of their loves. And though they might kill it, they
    wore
its pelt like a mantle
fallen upon them

from a vanishing form
after which they cried, as I cry, "My father, my father!"
But the figure had gone.
They are gone, too,

the lost and the lonely,
with Death, the dark nurse, who has dropped all their griefs in
    her pocket.
She comes so swiftly, even though
we wake up early.

Waiting

I leave my light burning
on the chance that you may come.
You have not come.
My light burns on the blackness
as an uprooted flower
floats on the water.

I sit alone waiting.
You absent, I want no other.
You have not come.
The minutes flake from the rock
of my solitude whence
I carve your face.

I leave my line open
on the chance that you may call.
You have not called.
The silence is only the sound
of my tongueless heart
crying your name.

I will not blame you.
It is not you who elect
the lapse of my pulse
for a leaf, the catch of my breath
for a shadow, my waiting
for no one at all.

Leave-Taking

You will not come for being called by all sweet names,
your lips long drifted into dust,
your breast dried to a bone,
your loins last quivered to a chill lost years ago
are hollowed honeycombs.
And so farewell
as I sit solitary in a crowd, feeling
the sharp edge unshared laughter has,
the loneliness of love endured
alone, with all the chatter stealing from me
even the silence.
And so farewell
as now tiptoe at the edge of myself,
light with drinking the wind, I sway
over the darkness of your face, dark cheek of the moon,
flower of darkness,
and no farewell.

Honest Confession

Do not wake before you will,
Do not come until you please.
Waiting for you gives me skill
In remaining at my ease.

If we never meet again
And I am not blessed by seeing
You once more, yet my life can
Be the sweeter for your being.

For at this long last I find
What's not taught by book or art:
Out of sight's not out of mind,
Out of mind is in your heart.

For I know away from me
You make music of the air
Like the solitary tree
Falling far from any ear.

Thus I boast where many another
Owned to ignorance long ago—
Till, as now we leave each other,
Tears confess I do not know.

The One Advantage

The wrestle with an angel's
No struggle with a ghost,
A ghost who can confer no names
And whose own name is lost.

Lacking a prior birth,
The second one aborts.
Old Adam cannot die without
A body to turn corpse.

You cannot walk on water
If you can't stand on stone.
You cannot speak in other tongues
Until you've learned your own.

Dodging past Yes and No,
You, therefore, can live free,
Kept hidden from both life and death
Beneath nonentity.

From an Old Maid

You come and say that it is restful here
to speak your pain into my silences,
wafting your words across them like the hair
of drowning sailors lost in churning seas.

And if I ever told you, you would laugh
to think I made your moment's reef of calm
by holding up your listless body, half
submerged in water, lightly on my palm.

Digging into my flesh with terror's claws
until the times you hope you hear the oar
of your salvation, do you never pause
to wonder when or where I drift to shore?

Complaint

Though you elude my leash of love,
my cage of care,
my net of need
so deftly that you keep your flight
a secret from yourself—
yet in your gracious circles you entwine me
whose spinning head follows your swift darting
till I fall dizzy,
caught captive in such freedom,
as the damned are trapped,
all tumbling down the bottomless abyss,
a flock of birds flying the boundless skies
of their full liberty
to go to Hell.

Love Song Minus Words and Music

For lulling this child
on the pulse of your gentleness,
too old for gentleness of your pulse;

for letting its head
lie down, if only for a moment,
within the shadow of your quietude;

for letting your words
speak to its wordlessness, your lips
improvising for it an echo—

this child whose form only
your eyes evoke is innocent
of how to insult you with thanks

save by its tears falling
into your hands like flowers withered
too long for the touch of the sun.

Warning

It was not much to do:
the flames of my sacrifice
were so small, they might have felt like a
    flicker of wind
in a martyr's holocaust;
my scourging so light
might have fallen, a kiss
on his bloody back,
and my cross so weightless
might have been some curious craft
flirting with flight.
Yet, unregarded, my gnat's cry, nit's clamor
shall, like Gabriel's trumpet,
shatter your diamond panes.

Hope

Is there no end at all,
riding down the rope of the wind,
winding down into the pit of the self,
falling, falling, falling
toward the bottom of darkness,
save a ledge that the foot catches on
for a moment to let me
kneel on the rushes of prayer!
Yet under my knee
the knob of earth crumbles
down the dark shaft of air
toward the underground river of sleep,
where side by side may we float
after our sweet toil together,
scarcely touching, but drifting
out toward the sunlight—
double rose on one stem!

Elusive

Your heart beats under my hand like a bird,
like a bird I would hold in my hand,
yet if I could coop it there it would be you no longer
and like a most delicate bird would die.
But that music playing, those notes circling about me
like birds weaving an intricate ballet in air,
that music composed and made and heard by men who
    have never known you,
whom you do not know,
impersonal as birds and intimate as birds with themselves
(not being "he" and "she," but not being "it")—
that is most you.

Regret

Had you come to me
as I to you once
with naked asking,
I should have let you.
We should have slept,
two arrows bound together
wounding no one.
Instead, you chose to lie
set to the bow of your own darkness.

Protest

Where the air in this room warms by the fire like a cat,
where music no one can touch swaddles the ear in satin,
where one may hear words as though he were tasting them,
where wine curls over the tongue, sliding down like a
    lover's kiss,
where the merest shadow of love bears the odor of roses
in whose heart I am flayed as by fire,
here I lie naked, spitted upon my senses
like a plucked bird caught upon thorns.

At a Child's Baptism

For Sarah Elizabeth

Hold her softly, not for long
Love lies sleeping on your arm,
Shyer than a bird in song,
Quick to fly off in alarm.

It is well that you are wise,
Knowing she for whom you care
Is not yours as prey or prize,
No more to be owned than air.

To your wisdom you add grace,
Which will give your child release
From the ark of your embrace
That she may return with peace

Till she joins the elemental.
God Himself now holds your daughter
Softly, too, by this most gentle
Rein of all, this drop of water.

Letters to a Young Girl Considering a Religious Vocation

I

I hope that you are certain,
for if you are not, you will be
a baby playing with matches
and may burn up your whole world.
Soon you will find
that the cross is less often of wood
than of air, that the nails are the winds
whistling through the holes in your heart.
Since the cross is implied
in the shape of everybody,
do not say I presume
who wear no habit
but the habit of every day.
Where else but here have I learned
how well we do
to get through our lives alive!
So, I could wish for you
that there, where you are supposed to die,
you do not finish as merely
an extended death-gasp.
It would be a matter for weeping
were we to stand side by side
and not to be told apart
when dissected down to our cinders
that used to be souls.

II

After our applause,
harmless enough in itself,

31

after our envy,
not really malignant,
after our praise,
which, though it cannot carry you far,
cannot wreck you,
if you are determined to go—
may all of this cease
in a hush that is more than their echo
of a whining importunity
whereto you grimace and gesture
and writhe and gyrate
and wriggle and jump
in the postures of peace;
more than their elongation
of the shadow cast by a crone
clapping her toothless gums
stealing the name of silence.

Pilgrim Perplexed

Here in the desert of the day
or the marshes of monotony
or the flatlands of finitude
(the designation is indifferent,
because the geography is undistinguished)—
who would believe if I told him
how the air falls, a foot on my heart,
how the telephone coils, a black silent shadow,
how the light and the dark form the stripes
on the back of an invisible tiger,
crouching under the bed
and behind the tables and chairs?
Nor would anyone guess how you are my angel
here in this terrain, in this atmosphere
drunk on its very sobriety—
you, hair awry for a halo,
a cloud of dust doing for wings,
a stammering breath for a message
which you speak by a gesture
as all love speaks anyway, talking with its hands.
I myself can scarcely conceive
here where prayer is no more
than a set mouth and clenched teeth,
and every presence fleshed in an absence,
how your eyes hold reflected that vision
which is unbearable, being
the only one mortals can bear.

Witness for the Defense

Small flower turning toward the sun,
You turn to find your mother's breast.
So white, so helpless, so your own,
The Host within your hand may rest.

Hive, then, the honey of this hour
In your each cell and never wish,
When you grow wiser, that the flower
Of thought had not its roots in flesh

Whose substance caused by loving art
For a few moments more to linger
Soon melts to space, which forms its heart,
To balance on your spirit's finger.

In Love

You do not move to music,
yet in your presence sit my bones
singing in silence.
And if they sang aloud
for every one to hear
I should not care.

Sometimes on your subtlety
you wear obtuseness like a wart,
and you grow all rough edges
bruising my heart.
Yet if I catch and keep you in a tear,
I love my weeping.

Clumsy, yet most delicate
are you to take a word
and make of breath
a home, for were love not the name
of where I live, I would be nothing,
being nowhere.

Each After Its Own Kind

My weapons of words,
my battlements of breath,
my tactics of tears
I have laid aside.
I keep still
like a child
sitting upon the floor,
waiting.
I can do nothing
except acknowledge that you
are to be trusted
not to be stone and oak,
but to be wind and water,
washing both away.

Metamorphoses

You kissed her, and I watched you for a moment
bridled to your desire, tamed to the will of the woods,
to the way of the wilds, your urbane grace
skittish and shy compared to the creature come down to drink
    of her beauty by dusk.
And I thought for a moment how
my body might be other than itself—
its proper parts be banks whereon you rested,
groves wherein you sheltered, pastures where you pleasured,
my speaking be the flow and ravel of its lines
leaping, cascading, sharply declining downward,
opened into the pool of shadow wherein you dived at leisure.

And under your kiss that it could not feel
my flesh, dispassionate stick beside you, startled
back to its formal freedom.

The Perpetual Penitent

When every bright bird's song
becomes a hissing tongue,
when every leaf has laid
against his throat a blade,
when all the breezes spin
the dark yarn of his sin,
when grass shoots pins and needles
into his feet and wheedles
confessions from him, and
the air's a burning brand—
he asks from time to time
the nature of his crime,
whereon the skies, once shrill
to damn him, falling still,
their silence brings no cheer,
since he but blames his ear
for having some disease,
for which upon his knees
down life's long aisle he'll falter
toward a retreating altar
where, if by trying hard
he'd reach, his high reward
would be soon to exhaust
himself as holocaust.

Belated Lullaby

Your love and anger sweep
Into one tide of sleep
Past hearing, beyond seeing
Where you in your own being

Lulled by your own pulse beat,
Warmed by your own heart's heat—
Marry your own night, pollen
From your closed eyelids fallen,

Repose where your breath is
A coil of silences,
Recline where its release
Balances war and peace

In easy elegance
Where flesh and spirit dance,
Shadowing, bound yet free,
Bach's ordered ecstasy.

Caught in the Act

We ascertain your stone
Correctly set in place,
The grass around it mown
To an appropriate grace.

Such soft and senseless gestures
By persons of perspicience
Seemed all so many postures
For which you had no patience.

But even if you mock
We cannot catch your jeer,
And here we will come back
To you who are not here.

(Or so you'd have it said,
All tidy in your shroud,
Like a baby tucked in bed,
So proper and so proud.)

Me and Schweitzer

Little brown patches
pasted against the wall,
folded into the shadows—
moths are so fragile.

You say, "What was that?"
and it was only a moth,
fluttering whisper ticking
against a light bulb.

How can you bear to kill
one with a well-aimed newspaper
watch it fall like a leaf from a lampshade—
you as gentle as moths

crumpled upon
my pulse, rotting inside
my vein, their minute deaths
in my bone lively!

Or as Gertrude Stein Says...

The sky is as blue as itself,
and the tree is as green as its leaves.
How shall I write a poem about today?

The tree stands—
but the tree has no feet.
The tree leans its head—
but the tree is not tired,
growing without resting
resting without pausing.

Let me try again.

The wind blows.
How, having no whistle?
The wind sings.
How, having no tune?
The wind sighs.
How, having no heart?
Yet it is lovers who borrow
from the wind their softness and storms.

Well then, the wind moves.
How, having no body
but the motion of bodies?

When the sky is as blue as itself,
and the tree is as green as its leaves—
a poem is only
taking a child's downy skull
gently between your hands
and, with not so much breath as might
    startle a gnat's wing,
whispering,
"Look!"

On Receiving a Philosopher's Autograph

Your ponderousness is nimbler than our nets;
you under your absurd weight outleap
our cleverest catches, dancing elephant;
in and out of your latinities you scuttle, squirrel,
hiding your nuts of meaning, which if we found them,
our dull teeth could not crack them, which keep you alive
and lively. Under our wariest watch you change your colors,
but keep your true one secret, shrewd chameleon.
You'll not be caught nor caged, and if defined,
you'll shed the definitions as a snake its skins.
Making such names for you is blowing bubbles
which burst the instant that we touch them.
Yet if we've caught one lesson, it is this—
we do not hold the wind, the wind holds us—
or so I felt that day you turned to me
and for the moment while you signed your name
gave all your substance in your shadow.

The End and the Beginning

Not knowing your address, I write you this letter
on the blank sheet of my breath
with the invisible ink of the wind
in the script of my tears:

Not knowing where you live, I say . . .
But who knows
where anyone lives?

Therefore,

Dear Love,
We flow through one another's fingers like drops of water!
We fly through the halls of one another's hearts into the night.
Remember, my love,
how you lit on my palm for a moment
and then were gone.
And my flesh you may happen to touch is only a feather
sprinkled and spelled by the salt of a moment's magic.
Your body is fresh and as firm as an apple;
its parts that I stroke like a child fingering her rosary—
from your face which rises upon my mornings instead of the sun
and enlightens my gloom more than the moonlight
down to the bright hairs webbed dark as a secret folded upon
    itself like a flower—
are only a shadow in which you lie hidden.
My own shape is the shade of a bubble
blown till it bursts out of your sight.
My love, tell me, then,
spilling at last out of each other's hands
fluttering helplessly like the broken wings of a bird,
will God gather us up?

The Ghostly Beast

My broken bones cry out for love
To bind me tighter than a glove,
Whereas I scarcely feel your hand
Bestowing what my bones demand.

I have no origin nor end
Within your heart's deep night unpenned;
You pick me up to set me down
Where I in seas of freedom drown.

Your weight withdrawn weighs burdensome
Upon my flesh till I become
The interval between two breaths,
A life lived out in little deaths.

Your airy fingers rub me raw
More than wolf's fang or tiger's claw;
The shadows of your passing rip
Skin from my body like a whip.

Distilling dew into a wine,
You make me grosser than a swine;
You feast me on platonic fare
Until I turn into a bear.

Though my protest may be no crisper
In your dominions than a whisper,
In rhymes like catapulted stones
My love cries out for broken bones.

Evensong

"Lighten our darkness, we beseech thee, O Lord";
for it is deep, this darkness that we wake to,
or go to sleep in.
It makes small difference
whether we say this prayer
at night or in the morning.
Are the darkness and the light both alike to thee, O Lord?
So are they to us, blind moles who burrow in the dust of the air.
"And by thy great mercy defend us from all perils and dangers
        of this night,"
of this night. We are precise.
Not of the night shaken by campfire and candle.
Not of the night scared off by electric light bulb and
        fluorescence,
but of the night never touched by the sunlight,
the night that is everyman's heart,
huge vine, running wild,
whose tendrils entrap us.
"For the love of thy Son, our Savior, Jesus Christ,"
of Him, mirror of God and Man.
But of us! Alas, O Lord,
we poor ghosts stand before a mirror,
wasting the waters of our images,
pouring them into
a glass without a bottom!

Easter Eve: A Fantasy

The day does not speak above a whisper, is a high dividing
upon a moment into ebbing and flowing,
two pairs of lips neither pressing nor quite yet parting,
the twilight between sleep and waking,
the bowl of hush held lifted to the bird's first trilling.
Yet the day does not wait. It has become a waiting
as we have become our shadows stuffed full of wind and
        walking,
and if my hand reached toward you, it would pass through you.
For the world has become a dream of that sleeping Head
which on Friday we pierced and folded in dust
until He awakens tomorrow when the light of His Rising
hardens to hills and crystallizes to rocks and ripples to streams.

My Bones Being Wiser

A eucharistic meditation

At Thy Word
my mind may wander,
but my bones worship
beneath the dark waters of my blood
whose scavenger fish
have picked them clean.

Upon them
Thy laws are written,
Thy days are notched,
and against the soreness of my flesh
they cry out the Creed
crossing themselves

against the cold,
huddled together,
rubbing themselves,
taking the posture of penitence,
warmed with the breath
of Thy absolution.

My eyes weep,
my heart refuses
to lift its head.
Still at Thy Comfortable Words
my bones, thrice deniers, stretch high, singing
a triple holy.

They would keep,
if not their joy
at least their sorrow
secret, but lie on Thy altar,
a bundle of faggots
ready for burning.

My flesh is
the shadow of pride
cast by my bones
at whose core lies cradled a child tender
and terrible, like
the Lamb he prays

to have mercy,
lest the hands held up
fall empty, lest
the light-as-air Host be only air.
Yet the Child within
my bones knows better.

Though the dews of
thanksgiving never
revive my mind, my heart, or my flesh—
    my blest bones dance
out the door with glory
worn inside out.

A Dream from the Dark Night

Not a single one of Teresa's letters to John of the Cross remains. One day he suddenly said to one of his brethren that there was still one thing to which he was attached. From a sack he brought out paper after paper covered with firm, graceful handwriting, and burned them. They were the letters of Teresa of Jesus.—MARCELLE AUCLAIR, *Teresa of Avila*

Sometimes when the silence howls in my head
till I can hear nothing else,
when it would drown out discourse and music
(were I suffered to hear them)
here in the swirling sand dunes
where the only word spoken
cries at the quick of the heart,
where images, mind's alabaster and ivory
blow away into dust—
her script as rare as a necklace of ash,
fine as a lizard's footprint,
vital as tendrils veining white walls of her cells
I remember as one sucks a stone
and so take them and burn them
while I turn to You, O my God, my bruised feet
leaping the meadows of Your flesh
to the desert of darkness
where Your silence speaks so loud
I cannot hear You.

Self-Ordained

Lithe shadows flickering across a rock
Flashed the expressions of his face, the heir
Of heretic and rebel, forged from shock
Of lust dark in some granite-tufted lair.
I watched him kneel down like a buckled rod
Over his darkness gathered in a gulf,
An upstart Jacob wrestling with his God
Or some inflated image of himself,
Or both, who knows? His words dropped blazing brands
Upon injustice, which, smoked out, still lingers.
But as he lifted proud and angry hands
I saw the victims dangling from his fingers.
Then I remembered what his Master said
Of wheat and tares, and mildly bowed my head.

Judas

Always I lay upon the brink of love,
Impotent, waiting till the waters stirred,
And no one healed my weakness with a word;
For no words healed me without words to prove
My heart, which, when the kiss of Mary wove
His shroud, my tongueless anguish spurred
To cool dissent, and which, each time I heard
John whisper to Him, moaned but could not move.

While Peter deeply drowsed within love's deep
I cramped upon its margin, glad to share
The sop Christ gave me, yet its bitter bite
Dried up my ducts. Praise Peter, who could weep
His sin away, but never see me where
I hang, huge teardrop on the cheek of night.

Bedtime Prayer

Thank you for Holy Communion this morning,
although it was the ritual I enjoy most—
the bowing at the right time, the crossing myself at the
    right place,
missing no trick—
like a child with a new toy.
Thank You that I could visit my sick friend, Frances,
though she was such a bore that I felt rather good about it
till my feeling of goodness gave me a feeling of badness
and I was tossed to and fro on the pinpricks of pride and shame
like the Christian martyrs on the Roman spears
(but they at least knew whose martyrs they were, while I
    wasn't sure).
Thank You, too, that the masks are fixed back
on the face of my love and on mine,
although for a moment we had burst through them
as from the webs of a spider.
Naked and frightened our faces stared at each other,
ugly with sticky membrane still clinging about them.
But soon we spun them once more as though we were breathing
    them out.
Finally, thank You, O Lord, that I am so sleepy.
I thank You for this without reservation,
my need urging my gratitude, my gratitude urging my need,
ready to sink into sleep as a drowning man into water,
in whom, as both actor and audience,
his role is the real.

Spinster's Lullaby

For Jeff

Clinging to my breast, no stronger
Than a small snail snugly curled,
Safe a moment from the world,
Lullaby a little longer.

Wondering how one tiny human
Resting so, on toothpick knees
In my scraggly lap, gets ease,
I rejoice, no less a woman

With my nipples pinched and dumb
To your need whose one word's sucking.
Never mind, though. To my rocking
Nap a minute, find your thumb

While I gnaw a dream and nod
To the gracious sway that settles
Both our hearts, imperiled petals
Trembling on the pulse of God.

Trimming the Sails

I move among my pots and pans
That have no life except my own,
Nor warmth save from my flesh and bone,
That serve my tastes and not a man's.

I'm jealous of each plate and cup,
Frail symbol of my womanhood.
Creator-like, I call it good
And vow I will not give it up.

I move among my things and think
Of Woolman, who, for loving care
He had for slaves, used wooden ware,
And wash my silver in the sink,

Wishing my knives and forks were finer.
Though Lady Poverty won heart
Of Francis, her male counterpart
Would find in me a sad decliner.

Sometimes regret's old dogs will hound me
With feeble barks, yet my true love
Is Brother Fire and Sister Stove
And walls and friends and books around me.

Yet to renounce your high romances
Being part pain—may so to do
Prove half humility that you
May bless, good Woolman and sweet Francis!

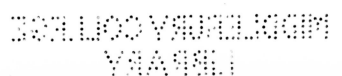

The One Thing Needful

"The cause of loving God is God alone,
And measure of this love there should be none."
Lest Bernard take my rhyming him amiss,
I'll tell him there's no poetry but this.

Therefore, young man, as good as debonair,
Who give your Gospel with so fine a flair,
I'd not quarrel with you on a single phrase
Save to remind you what St. Bernard says.

And more, "The Love that saved us from damnation
Saved angels from the need of such salvation."
Have you, I wonder, ever understood
Love so impartial perils platitude?

You tell us that since first you yielded up
Your all to God, he's overflowed your cup.
You give, God gives—so far a game God's won.
Who, after all, outplays the Champion?

I do not hint you'd not serve God for nought,
Nor from the malice whetted on such thought
Give theologians room to theorize
That Satan is a sorehead in disguise.

I'm certain that your grief-astounded gaze,
Adjusting, would dissolve to tears of praise.
For so did Francis's in rapt communion,
St. Joan of Arc's, blunt Luther's, and poor Bunyan's.

And Job himself, though he could not approve
God's justice, could do nothing else but love
As he could not help breathing, being hungry
For air, no less so when the air turned angry.

But still the love we have no right to measure
Concerns itself with neither pain nor pleasure.
What then? St. Bernard tells us. And there is,
God knows, no rhyme nor reason except his.

Carol of Brother Ass

In the barnyard of my bone
Let the animals kneel down—
Neither ecstasy nor anger,
Wrath nor mildness need hide longer,
On the branching veins together
Dove may sing with hawk her brother.

Let the river of my blood
Turned by star to golden flood
Be the wholesome radiance
Where the subtle fish may dance,
Where the only bait to bite
Dangles from the lures of light.

Let the deep angelic strain
Pierce the hollows of my brain;
Struck for want of better bell,
Every nerve grow musical;
Make my thews and sinews hum
And my tautened skin a drum.

Bend, astonished, haughty head
Ringing with the shepherds' tread;
Heart, suspended, rib to rib,
Rock the Christ Child in your crib,
Till so hidden, Love afresh
Lovely walks the world in flesh.

Renewal

I, like a stone
kneel while the waters
of prayer wash over me.

Like a hare havened
in its own stillness
I freeze against Thy whiteness.

Once more myself,
I feed upon
Thy manna of the minutes.

Bread-and-Butter Letter Not Sent

I crawl over myself
and, looking back over my shoulder,
surveying my fallen form,
mutter, "Aha!" like a mountain climber.

Popes and silly girls have visions,
but me, lost in the desert of myself,
Christ and His holy angels
have left severely alone.

Dear friend, in the swing of the sunlight
let me hold the knowledge of my pain
far away, like the sea in a shell
and wash my wounds for awhile in sleep.

I am sorry to sing you
no more melodious song, yet only
the taste of its notes biting my tongue reminds me,
sometimes, that I am alive.

Song for a Summer Afternoon

I look from my cage of cold
that hums like some sleepy monster
at the green trees waving over the tumble-down garage.
And the mourning dove mourns with the name of my long-lost
    love.

I hear the sparrows snipping pieces out of the hush,
I hear the cicadas murmur, voice of the silence,
of loneliness, invisible thread binding the years together.
And the mourning dove mourns with the name of my long-lost
    love.

I hear upon the thresholds of their cloudy kennels
the dogs of the thunder growling deep in their throats
as they strain at the yellow leashes of lightning.
And the mourning dove mourns with the name of my long-lost
    love.

All the summer days are one day, sick-sweet with the jasmine
    of yearning,
and I have grown neither taller nor older,
but only my shadow.
And the mourning dove mourns with the name of my long-lost
    love.

Peril

My words
beat at the cage of my bones
like birds.

Its door
never opened, bright wings strew
the floor.

My cries
catch in the web of my veins
like flies.

By art
they must escape that fat spider,
my heart.

Aubade

I press against the emptiness
and pray the air into a shape
which dreams will not shore up.

I listen to my next-door neighbor
scuffling about like a dry leaf.
She once had a body

like mine that, rotting with its ripeness,
falls from the branch of morning to
sullen floor of sleep.

Resolve

I must go back to the small place,
to the swept place,
to the still place,
to the silence under the drip of the dew,
under the beat of the bird's pulse,
under the whir of the gnat's wing,
to the silence under the absence of noise,
there bathe my hands and my heart
in the hush,
there rinse my ears and my eyes,
there know Thy voice and Thy face,
until when, O my God, do I knock
with motionless knuckles
on the crystal door of the air
hung on the hinge of the wind.

Commital

You are your own best news to me; so, speak
Or do not speak—the truth of you remains.
The lines that flow between us are not chains.
Such is my faith, although my faith is weak.

Let speaking be your silence, or your silence
Be speech, I try to trust. If I confess
My faith as feeble, it is faith no less
Begging your pardon to restore the balance—

A parable that God need never prove
Himself by being what we ask or think,
And if we test His waters when we drink,
Love smiles, yet will be nothing else but Love.

Loneliness

So deep is this silence
that the insects, the birds,
the talk of the neighbors in the distance,
the whir of the traffic, the music
are only its voices
and do not contradict it.

So deep is this crying
that the silence, the hush,
the quiet, the stillness, the not speaking,
the never hearing a word
are only the surge
of its innumerable waters.

This silence, this crying,
O my God, is my country
with Yours the sole footstep besides my own.
Save me amid its landscapes
so terrible, strange
I am almost in love with them!

Thank-You Note

You give this gift to me
A gift that cannot be
For me by right or grace,
Yet one I dare embrace.

For it will signify
The truth within a lie,
A token that, from you,
I may not keep, yet do.

Origin

By the thread of her singing
the bird poises silence
that will crush her.

I myself am that bird,
loneliness that silence,
hair-hung boulder.

Upon my bird's heart whetted,
the thought of you being
the blade, cuts it.

A Bird in the Hand

I do not feel the peace of the saints,
light fusing with darkness,
passing all understanding.

Nor yet the peace of the dead, who have drifted
beyond stir and stillness,
nothing to understand.

Mine, the catching of breath after pain,
the peace of those who have
almost died and still live.

I pray that the peace of God fall upon me;
the dead's comes unprayed;
but, for now, this suffices.

Contemplative

Blackbird folding her wings,
in the shade sits a nun
cool as a shadow,

yet a lens leashing the light
through its single eye, she
kindles the leaf

of our lives to flame,
just as, stiff as a stick,
day after day

she prays, washing with words
from her clear springs of singing
a dark world white.

Love's Eschatology

I touch you all over
as if every part were a petal
when now you are away.

Never has your body
before so budded to my senses
as to my empty fingers.

Love, may we in Heaven
view all for the first time forever
through the lens of the last.

Restraint

You are like water, which is
neither cold nor hot, tasting
only of itself.

Nothing else serves but water,
cool or warm, I do not care
I am so thirsty,

like a little child
who, yet, when you come sips warily
beyond his years,

more like men of the desert
who have always to keep one swallow
ahead of drouth,

or like penitents
with their lips brushing the chalice
more lightly than moths.

Note of Apology to Medea

A fluttered-down handkerchief,
so lightly she lies on the moot point
of resting or rising.

Now she eddies about,
a leaf in her own whirling, winding
the air in her brightness.

Her paws are like petals
and, although her claws are like thorns,
she means us no ill

when she mistakes our fingers
for the mouse of tomorrow, the catch
of her innocent cunning.

Enough, if by grace of such grace,
our smiles with no elsewhere to go
light on her who, all unbeholden,

lifts us and holds us a moment
in love's loop of laughter, a child's swing
shadowing turbulent waters.

Such frailty having borne
our burden even a second, how dare we
have named her Medea!

Minor Revelation

Like you, your notes may be
All inarticulate,
Yet show you think of me,
Hence calmly I await
Their coming whose intent
Is love's rich sacrament.

Smile at me, if you choose,
That I see allegory
Which for me does not lose
By being just the story
And homely parable
A child might think to tell:

God's secrets in a sign
None parses phrase by phrase,
For neither bread nor wine
Expounds to us His ways
In ways we can discuss—
Save that He thinks of us.

So, every hour I wake
I praise God that His wrath
Tempers for me who take
To Him this humblest path,
That He, indeed, insures
His mysteries in yours.

Casual

The grief that wears me now I will wear yet
cut to a pattern with pain's shears,
sown with a fine seam of sorrow,
stitched with tears,
fitted so snugly about me with sweat
till on that morrow
never a beauty shall go more proudly
in silk or satin, velvet or furs,
and, oh, such rich-rare stuffs no old maid mind dares name,
or with the flounce and flaunt of that body of hers
proclaim
more loudly
or with more shine,
"Mine!"
By which day grief turned into my skin,
nerve-shocked, bleeding if pricked by a pin,
something to buffet, tear up, or tug at,
will be merely a matter to shrug at
instead of a garment for shame or for pride.
Then maybe I can cast it aside
like some desert devotee who at a word
from the wind strips to his crazy bones
and over the steaming stones
dances before the Lord.

Promise

Some day I will put you all in a book:
You strict, you strange, you wizened and you wild,
You whole, you unholy ones whom I took
My lessons from the times I was a child;
You rock, that my heart always shattered upon,
You, bruising as you slipped my fingers, water,
When sometimes rock melts and water turns stone
And which is which not seldom doesn't matter,
Because love forever comes toward us naked
Of every name, yet answering to any,
Or multimasked, looking wistful and wicked,
Brilliant and brooding, furious and funny.
Including me, this book, this temporal Heaven
Squaring the circle, makes it oddly even.

Decision

You will not return for my tears,
Nor come to my call,
And whether for days or for years
Does not matter at all,

Since sometimes a moment's too long,
Or a day's too short.
What measures the length of a song?
Not the clock but the heart.

Not being the first one to lean
Beyond hope and dread,
For no rain has kept the earth green
But the tears of the dead

And the quick. So comforted (dafter
Than some) for awhile
At least, I lie down on soft laughter
In the curve of a smile.

Taunt-Song

I hear you calling, but I do not come.
I cannot? Will not? A small difference.
Though once my every nerve would have been tense,
My body all an ear—when you were dumb.

I hear you call, but a great gulf appears
Between us such as angels will to fix,
Or furies, and whether Jordan or the Styx
Is but its shadow or its shadow theirs,

I do not know, but although you may shout
Me up and down the ways of the whole world,
I, hermit crab, here hidden, freed and furled
Within herself, need not go in or out.

Thorn in the Flesh

Light comes again
but sometimes
falls at crooked angles.

Now there is song,
but sometimes
the silence conducts it.

My days are full
but sometimes
only of your absence.

I have been healed,
but sometimes
still the whole heart hobbles.

Regression

Morning I walk tall
when darkness twitched from my shoulder
scampers to hide, a drowsy froglet,
snippet of night left over in the hedges.

Evenings, though, my shadow
lengthening, my shadow dwindling
to crawl inside itself and curl up tight
squirms, a damp baby in a soggy blanket.

Pilgrim Song

My love so wild and sweet like wind or flowing water,
I would pursue, and yet by running after
in all directions but pivot on one point.

My child so wild and sweet like wind or flowing water,
whose mother I am not nor yet your father,
you fly my keeping, and I freeze to chase you.

My God, so wild and sweet, like wind or flowing water,
I cannot hold in head or heart or hand,
yet seeking to, am with You three-in-one.

Note to the Reader

This book, these sheets of paper you pick up
And toss aside for being only ink—
This is soul's sweat and bile, black slag, outcrop
Of heart's New England, apples of its stone.
I loafed to write it, but, how toilingly
Prone on the earth and felt it knock
Hard on my breasts and belly, needling me
With grass for fingers, muttering, "Unlock!"
It may be luxury that wind has mussed
My skirt and blouse, to coax my body bare,
Or that my maid's the wind, my suitor's dust,
My bed and boudoir everywhere nowhere.
Yes, call it ease—but name my book's each word
What angels flask to pour before their Lord!

Acknowledgement

I walk with my head in the air.
For if I look below,
God, Thou art also there.
Lord, how far must I go
Down on my knees in likeness,
A little, of Thy meekness.

I walk with my head held all proud.
Ashamed to look shamefaced,
I cry my worth aloud,
Since God alone is graced
With lowliness, till I stumble
Over the Most High humble.

Lord, dare I crawl on my knees?
I find Thy cross thereunder,
My ease is my unease,
Thy whisper strikes with thunder
Thy poor competitor
Meek but by metaphor.

Distinguished books of contemporary poetry
available in cloth-bound and paperback editions
published by Wesleyan University Press

Alan Ansen:	*Disorderly Houses* (1961)
John Ashbery:	*The Tennis Court Oath* (1962)
Robert Bagg:	*Madonna of the Cello* (1961)
Robert Bly:	*Silence in the Snowy Fields* (1962)
Donald Davie:	*New and Selected Poems* (1961)
James Dickey:	*Drowning With Others* (1962)
David Ferry:	*On the Way to the Island* (1960)
Robert Francis:	*The Orb Weaver* (1960)
Richard Howard:	*Quantities* (1962)
Barbara Howes:	*Light and Dark* (1959)
David Ignatow:	*Say Pardon* (1961)
Donald Justice:	*The Summer Anniversaries* (1960)
	(A Lamont Poetry Selection)
Chester Kallman:	*Absent and Present* (1963)
Vassar Miller:	*My Bones Being Wiser* (1963)
Vassar Miller:	*Wage War on Silence* (1960)
Hyam Plutzik:	*Apples from Shinar* (1959)
Louis Simpson:	*At the End of the Open Road* (1963)
Louis Simpson:	*A Dream of Governors* (1959)
James Wright:	*The Branch Will Not Break* (1963)
James Wright:	*Saint Judas* (1959)

FEB 1 2 1965

1/24/64